MILWAUKEE Scavenger

Jenna Kashou

Copyright © 2022 by Reedy Press, LLC
Reedy Press
PO Box 5131
St. Louis, MO 63139, USA
www.reedypress.com

Library of Congress Control Number: 2022937091

ISBN: 9781681064017

Cover and interior design by Claire Ford

Front cover and interior photos by the author. Back cover headshot by Uttke Photography. Interior clip art courtesy of Pixabay and Wikimedia Commons.

Printed in the United States of America
22 23 24 25 26 5 4 3 2 1

Dedication

This book would not have been possible without my husband Ramsey, who has taken me on the most true and exciting adventure. Plus, there isn't a puzzle he couldn't solve or a riddle he couldn't write with his spunky prose.

Cash and Ruby, my children, have been little rays of sunshine these past two years while the world has been in crisis. Together, we practice presence and resilience, as best we can, every day! I thank them for bringing so much joy to my life.

Contents

Acknowledgments

Every resident has their own version of Milwaukee based on the familiar places they live, work, and play. But there's always an opportunity to rediscover different parts of the city with an open heart and open mind.

I will forever be optimistic about our city's possibility based on the civic and community leaders that I have met. After all, good leadership is always the key to success. I see inspired, collaborative and caring people every day with an intense desire to see their neighbors thrive. This selfless leadership makes Milwaukee a wonderful city to raise a family and build a career.

Hospitality and tourism leaders from MMAC and VISIT, Milwaukee, and representatives of the various neighborhood associations—you are the absolute best cheerleaders for our city. Small business owners, you share your talents to make our city unique, so thank you for your determination and dedication.

We've seen a lot of milestones for the city in the past two years. Two that I am most excited about are our first (and youngest) Black mayor, Cavalier Johnson, and our first Latino Common Council President, Jose Perez. Our city's racial, cultural, and ethnic diversity makes it special, and now our leadership reflects that.

I hope you'll enjoy the thrill of this scavenger hunt as much as I have and gain a new appreciation for our fine city. Now get out and #Explore_the_414!

Introduction

Flying high from a 2021 NBA Championship, Milwaukee is the underdog no more! Just five years ago, we were in jeopardy of losing our NBA team. That's just one example of this city's perseverance. But more than grit, Milwaukee has heart. Neighbors take care of one another and we support local businesses. We fly "414" flags and wear all sorts of funny (locally made) Milwaukee-themed tees to show our civic pride. As they say ... "There's always good things brewing in Milwaukee!"

While we do embrace the beer, brat, and cheese culture very well, there is so much more to Milwaukee. This book will help you appreciate and uncover historical buildings, natural wonders, dazzling works of art, and new hot spots.

The thrill of the hunt is a hard feeling to encapsulate, but I trust, since you're reading this book, that you love the thrill, too. Explore each neighborhood by foot or bike to get the best vantage point. Each chapter is designed so that people new to the neighborhood can walk and find most of the clues in close proximity. And be sure to check out the chapter on Milwaukee's streetcar, The Hop. All of the spots can be seen while riding on the M-line—a great family activity for a rainy day!

Think you can find them all? Enter your answers on mkescavenger.com for your chance to win prizes from local sponsor Sendik's Food Market and more.

I am certain you will find much more than the answers to these clues along the way. Now, get out and #Explore_the_414!

Legend

Shorewood

This bustling suburb just north of Milwaukee is residential, but it's also filled with shops, bars, and places to grab a bite. Stately old homes line the streets off of the lakefront and over 100 stairs descend to the idyllic Atwater Beach, which rivals any other coast and is favored by Midwestern surfers. Start your journey on Lake Drive.

1

Hidden trail reveals a natural gem,
Discover a mix of leaves, sticks, and stems.
Descend the long, steep hill with ease;
Warning: the walk up is not a breeze.

2

Look for the spot marking wreckage below,
Not to be seen as it is not shallow.
Long ago, on a mission to deliver coal,
Sadly, this wooden vessel never met its goal.

3

Steel letters are the tools for experiencing the world;
They're stacked into a form, illuminated and curled.
It watches over the horizon and once caused a stir,
Altered so controversy it would never again spur.

4

This is a place of learning, worship, and ritual,
See Romanesque style like arches, continual,
You could see a couple in wedded bliss,
The lofty bell tower is a hard one to miss.

5

Want to learn all about things French?
Get in the game: stop warming that bench.
It's cheaper than a plane ticket to Paris,
Take classes here, no need to be an heiress.

6

At this spot, put your musical skills to the test,
Learn how to play, perform, and be your best.
If you've dreamed of being Springsteen or Bowie,
Remember to practice, and don't get too showy.

7

This place is perfect for the biggest beer snob,
Especially if you think drinking is actually your job.
There's always something new to wet your whistle,
They even have a beer school, but no early dismissal!

8

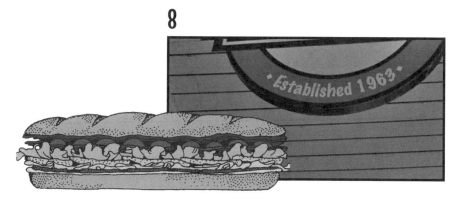

Finally, a legit deli, in the style of New York,
But whatever you do, don't ask for pork.
It's kosher, but definitely not for vegans;
Try the corned beef, for so many reasons.

9

This train takes to the track twice a night,
Named after an apparition that causes fright.
Is it real or just a figment of your imagination?
It has traveled 400 miles to reach its destination.

10

It's a white, historic house that goes by two names;
A fabulous collection of art and antiques, it contains.
It was moved to this popular park to save from ruin,
Walk further into the park to find something brewin'.

_____

_____

11

Looking for a rustic, tasty brunch?
Like to hang at a beer garden for lunch?
Enjoy this cozy spot by the river;
With outdoor domes so you won't shiver.

_____

_____

Riverwest

Riverwest is like no other neighborhood in Milwaukee. It's a quirky, diverse, and tight-knit community, home to many artists. Famous for its 24-hour bike ride and block party in July, there are plenty of green spaces and bike lanes. The nightlife scene cannot be matched, with everything from a psychedelic dance club and tiki bar to corner pubs hosting open mic nights and national acts. Start your tour on Humboldt Boulevard.

Even if you don't have a green thumb,
Make a green oasis, without feeling dumb.
This shop has live greens of every variety;
They throw in advice to cure your anxiety.

2

A corner tavern with much more than beer,
Watch people play volleyball most of the year.
Our wacky weather is why we're so hearty,
Especially when it's time to drink and to party.

3

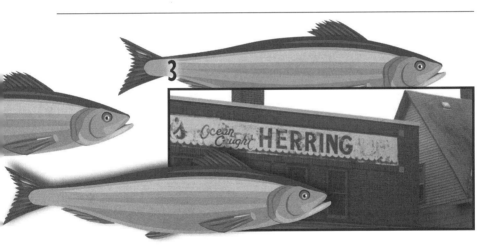

A family biz whose slogan's "The kiss of health,"
After all, it's considered your greatest wealth.
Some called the salty treat an acquired taste,
A spin on a tradition that's Scandinavian-based.

4

A rustic craft brewery named after a dog,
Imbibe too much and you'll end up in a fog.
Bring your four-legged friend along for a drink,
Some say it's better therapy than using a shrink.

5

If you love literature, this spot is for you,
With performances and words are read aloud, too.
Locally run, focused on all things independent,
It's the place for an experience that's transcendent.

6

At this sprawling green space
Kids play, climb, and race.
In the summer the grills are hot;
Running through fountains, children trot.

7

If a tropical drink is something you crave,
This haunt is kitschy and dark as a cave.
The flaming Tiki Love Bowl is nothing to fear;
A few sips and you're grinning, ear to ear.

8

At the center is love for Italian food,
We all know that carbs improve your mood.
The ambience is perfect for a first date:
Have an app and dessert, or share a plate.

9

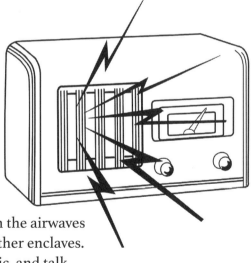

A channel for the community on the airwaves
For those in Riverwest, and all other enclaves.
Hear true stories, opinions, music, and talk,
Observe the operation while out for a walk.

10

Unique work by local artists decorates the walls
At this fav watering hole; there's also pinballs,
Plus pool tables, darts, pizza, and more,
That's why it's a spot that locals adore.

11

A place of worship, originally for the Polish,
The doors are flanked by two towers, quite tallish,
It welcomes all people, no matter their creed;
Over 100 years old, it helps do good deeds.

12

Locally grown food that comes from the heart,
Margaritas and queso are a good way to start.
They're so popular, they've started to expand,
Their Mexican dishes are anything but bland.

13

This paved path borders an old rail line,
Great for bikes, walking, and leisure time.
Bordering where breweries were constructed,
Lush with foliage, city views are obstructed.

14

A bright and cheery spot for a break or a rest,
Chock-full of art, pick which you like best.
This park is well-suited for kids' creative play:
Look closely when you drive by; it's hidden away.

15

A place where arias are staged and rehearsed,
These singers and performers are very well-versed.
The historic building is classic Cream City brick,
When selecting what to see, it's hard to pick.

16

I hope you wore your dancing shoes,
The best way to shake off the blues.
Windowless mass of yellow bricks
A funky music spot. Great pick!

17

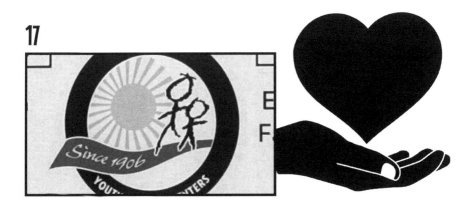

A place where kids and families thrive;
The park beside hosts music, live.
Aftercare and preschool stages;
Program works when town engages.

A shop filled with stuff so quirky and fun;
Its gifts, toys, and games delight everyone.
The bold storefront's a bright spot on the street,
The owner is welcoming to everyone she meets.

_____

_____

Brewer's Hill/ Beerline District

Looking for a spectacular view of the city? Head to Historic Brewer's Hill, which sits atop a bluff over the Milwaukee River. This once mainly residential area housed workers at the foundries, tanneries, mills, and breweries that lined the river. Now, people flock to this neighborhood for cafes, parks, and craft beer. Start your trek on Commerce Street.

1

This charming cafe's menu can't be be beat,
It's all handmade, and not a shred of meat.
There are lots of options to fill your plate:
Who knew that just plants could satiate?

2

Climb this flight to reach the park on the hill,
Seven steel frames create artwork, sans frills.
This structure connects two neighborhoods
Where the first industrial giants once stood.

3

Like a mammal who carries her young in a pouch,
This walkway's expansive, you won't have to crouch.
An urban plaza of wood, concrete, and steel,
Commuters are welcome, both on foot and two wheels.

4

The city's first craft operation to sling brews,
The tour's famous, if you ain't heard the news.
Outside, tanks are painted like Larry, Curly, and Moe,
Friday night fish fry and polka are a must-go.

5

If a hearty breakfast or brunch you seek,
Look for the corner spot with a boutique.
Beautifully appointed and lovingly restored,
The ever-changing menu won't leave you bored.

6

A church and school known for its excellence,
Here they worship a figure of eminence.
The huge red brick edifice, built in 1913,
Was here long before kids studied on screens.

_____

_____

7

Performance space in a park on a hill,
It's a perfect spot to hang out and chill.
Indulge in Shakespeare or Salsa tunes
Or explore on a lazy afternoon.

_____

_____

Bronzeville/Schlitz Park

Along the Milwaukee River, Schlitz Park is home to the former Milwaukee brewer with the tagline: "The Beer That Made Milwaukee Famous." Historic buildings now house businesses focusing on enlivening the community. The adjacent Bronzeville neighborhood flourished as the arts and culture center of the city in the 1950s. It celebrated (and still does) African American culture. Revitalization efforts are underway, with unique local businesses opening all the time. Start at Second and Cherry streets as you make your way over to Martin Luther King Boulevard.

1

This bright work of art depicts a classic local scene
From back when the Milwaukee River was much more clean,
Bringing new life to the district that used to make beer,
Now it's is great place to start a new career.

2

School is named for a teacher and Israeli politician
Whose work in Milwaukee was the start of her mission.
She once attended the school that now bears her name
Before she moved on and achieved so much fame.

3

Young musicians and actors flock to this space
To rehearse and perform, a smile on their face.
Arts education builds life skills for our youth,
You can argue if you want, but that's the truth!

4

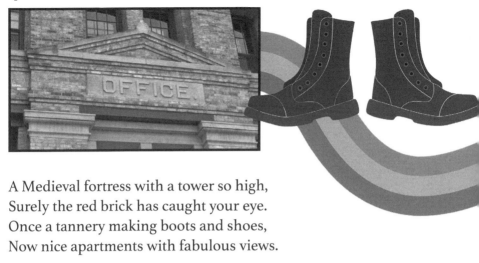

A Medieval fortress with a tower so high,
Surely the red brick has caught your eye.
Once a tannery making boots and shoes,
Now nice apartments with fabulous views.

_____

_____

5

Historically, a place where the horses would board.
To see a pair of horse heads, tilt your head skyward.
Like its neighbors, the building is made from cream brick,
Now used as an office, find people moving around quick.

_____

_____

6

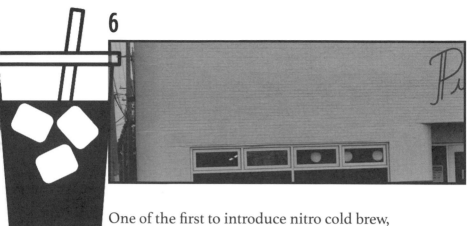

One of the first to introduce nitro cold brew,
Smooth, creamy, and so thick you could almost chew,
Its red-branded tasting room catches your eye;
For "java junkies," their blends can give you a high.

7

It's kind of like sausage, but more like . . . meat jelly?
You won't find this family recipe in any old deli.
Really, just what is headcheese, anyway?
Give it a try: you might just be blown away.

8

If you're looking for two wheels,
This spot has the very best deals.
Here, they teach teens how to work,
Which is just one of the many perks.

_____

_____

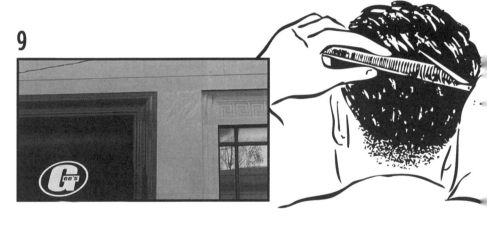

9

For 25 years, this barber's the real deal:
See how good a fresh look can make you feel.
Let them give you a trim, a fade, or buzz cut,
Walk out with confidence; show us your strut.

_____

_____

10

It's historical and a memorial for Blacks,
Before this place, information lacked.
You'll see how people suffered, just like the Jews,
These historical events are too important to lose.

_____

_____

11

Civil Rights leader, this street bears his name,
Making contributions, apart from his fame.
Looking proud atop books cast in bronze;
Take a better selfie than with the Fonz.

_____

_____

Lindsey Heights/ Sherman Park

Sherman Park is one of Milwaukee's oldest and largest neighborhoods. This area on the northwest side is a leader in urban farming, community organizing, and wellness trends. Both Lindsey Heights and Sherman Park have a renewed focus on building strong, healthy communities after many years of turmoil. Start at North Avenue as you work your way north.

1

A Milwaukee institution since 1955,
Many would argue it's worth the drive.
Hot, hand-cut pastrami or tasty corned beef,
A classic deli lives on: what a relief!

2

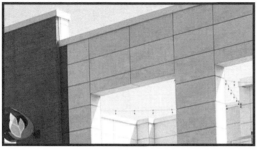

This community cafe serves food healthy and tasty,
Although it's carryout, no need to be hasty.
This here's an oasis to learn about food
While teaching entrepreneurs how to be shrewd.

_____

_____

3

Create community, innovate, and care for the earth,
Build gardens and parks; remind people of their worth.
Spur economic development: collaboration is key!
Discover the type of community you want to see.

_____

_____

4

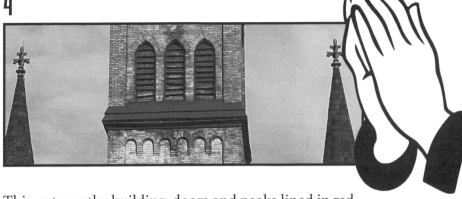

This noteworthy building, doors and peaks lined in red,
Where followers worship and clear their heads,
This facade's been a mainstay for o'er 65 years,
Teaching Christian values and soothing people's fears.

5

Teaching children in kindergarten up through grade five,
Mixing academics and enrichment so children can thrive,
Outfitting the next brave community leaders
With interpersonal skills, and creating good readers.

6

This huge urban farm has roots that run deep,
Traditions, both food and cultural, they keep.
Agricultural enterprise and holistic health
Come together, so people can create wealth.

_____

_____

7

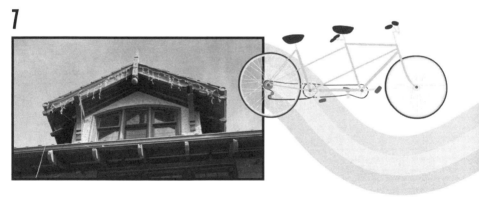

In a historic tavern, this restaurant on a mission
Provides on-the-job training for those with ambition
With seasonal family recipes, made from scratch;
The chef was handed the restaurant: what a good match.

_____

_____

8

The only public park in Lindsey Heights
Got a major face-lift, including more lights.
Progress, when community comes together,
Ensuring this space to play is much better.

_____

_____

9

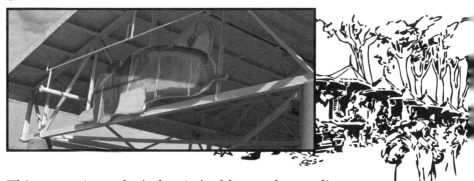

This open-air market's the city's oldest and most diverse,
A place to meet people and farmers' goods to disperse,
Supporting family farmers and improving fresh food access;
With volunteers, larger community issues it can address.

_____

_____

10

Risen from the ashes, the site of violent protests,
This former bank houses businesses finding success.
Find food and herbs, services and art,
Community leaders knew this would be smart.

11

Perk up at this quaint, nostalgic shop,
Where diverse community members stop.
It shares its name with the neighborhood
And also a war general who did good.

Upper East Side

Home to expansive parks, historic and grand homes, a nationally recognized university, restaurants, shops, and theaters, the Upper East Side really has it all. Students and University of Wisconsin-Milwaukee community members live in cozy pockets of homes while enjoying both on- and off-campus amenities, with Lake Michigan just minutes away. Start on Oakland Avenue and head south.

1

This family-owned spot serves Italian fare,
Their pizza's to die for: just order a pair.
The crust's thin and crispy, toppings are generous;
Try tuna or anchovies, if you're feeling adventurous.

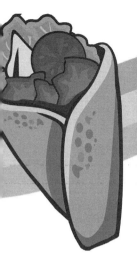

2

Packed late-night, its customers satiated,
Greek food just tastes better when you're inebriated.
This spot is a staple at "Oak and Loc,"
The cheap, casual vibe is perfect if you're broke.

3

A place for musicians to share their talents onstage
Some nights it's a dance club where people can rage.
Cheap drink specials draw the college crowd,
Just like many music venues: it's dark and loud!

4

Past the playground in this park is a nature-lover's paradise,
With ways to enjoy the outdoors when city life won't suffice.
There's a building situated right on the riverbanks,
The trails and special programs will have you giving thanks.

5

Inside of Lake Park, there's a sport like bocce ball,
But this game you can only play through the fall.
Outside, roll colorful balls along fresh-mowed grass;
If you want to learn how to play, they offer a class.

6

In Milwaukee's first public park, eight beasts stand guard,
But don't fear, they're not real: they're limestone and hard.
At either end of two southern bridges, they look proud;
To the city of MKE, these sculptures were endowed.

_____

_____

7

Across the park's bridge stands a towering work of art,
The bronze sculpture commemorates a man with heart,
A prominent Wisconsin leader during Civil War times,
Always ready to lead the charge; on his horse he climbs.

_____

_____

8

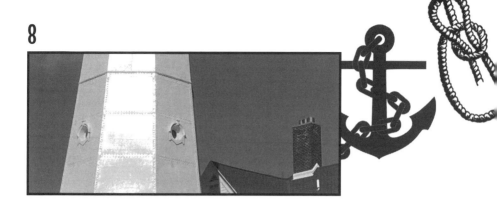

Maritime artifacts in this tall, thin museum,
Maintaining it's an effort that's Herculean.
Once operational, it helped ships find their way;
This historical landmark, an attraction will stay.

9

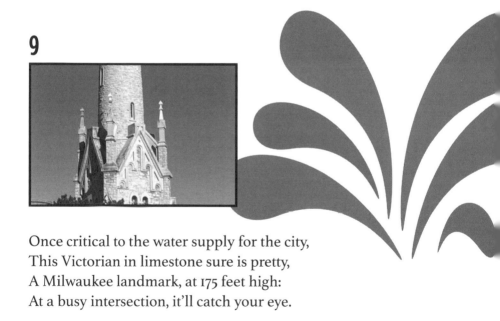

Once critical to the water supply for the city,
This Victorian in limestone sure is pretty,
A Milwaukee landmark, at 175 feet high:
At a busy intersection, it'll catch your eye.

10

The original cafe celebrating bikes and beer,
A great place for Sunday brunch to kick into gear,
Known for their frites and food with Dutch flair,
Relax on the patio and enjoy some fresh air.

11

It's the place for literary events, inspo and gifts,
You can read here or find help writing your own riffs.
Independent and locally-owned: rare these days,
Oh, how I love reading, let me count the ways!

12

The oldest place in MKE to catch a flick,
Chairs swathed in red velvet are cushy and thick,
The marquee boasts indie and foreign titles,
Cultural gems like this in our city are vital.

13

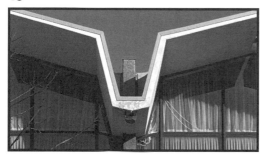

The central spot for the university community,
The halls are filled with plenty of opportunity.
There's an art gallery, cinema, rec center, and more,
And pick up some swag at the Panther store.

14

While on campus, stop here for a concert.
Enjoy a break from reality, and divert
Your attention with an orchestra, theatre, or dance;
The audience applauds, their lives are enhanced.

15

It should be on water, but it's found on land;
At its bow, a lighthouse replica stands.
Since 1920, a house on the East Side,
Through Airbnb, you can stay inside.

Lower East Side

The Lower East Side is chock-full of interesting places to eat, drink, and experience. Historic Brady Street, first settled by Italian immigrants, is now the place to go for a wild weekend. Smaller museums line Prospect Avenue and street art is anything but sparse on Farwell Avenue. With just a quick jaunt down one of the many hills, you're at the Lakefront. Start on Prospect Avenue and head north, before you loop back on Farwell and head down to Brady Street.

1

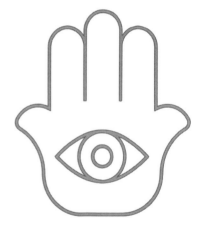

A place dedicated to the Jewish experience away from home,
Hosting exhibits and telling stories less-known,
Preserving everything from photos, art, letters, and clothes
Archives date back to the 1800s: all the highs and lows.

2

Fine musical instruction, all genres and ages;
Don't be intimidated, you'll learn it in stages,
A great spot to enjoy a live concert from the pros,
Providing music for schools and prepping for shows.

_____

_____

3

This 1900s mansion is an Eschweiler gem,
Featuring a couple's collection of what's special to them.
See their interesting artifacts, pottery, and more,
And special exhibits for you to explore.

_____

_____

4

A full-service restaurant, deli, and more,
Plus specialty groceries and gifts in the store.
It began as a health food store for veg-heads;
Funny how new food and diet trends spread.

_____

_____

5

PROST!

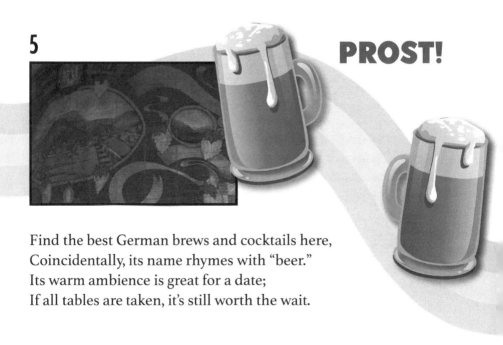

Find the best German brews and cocktails here,
Coincidentally, its name rhymes with "beer."
Its warm ambience is great for a date;
If all tables are taken, it's still worth the wait.

_____

_____

6

An ornate home for indies and East Indian decor,
Though the room is dark, it's not polite to snore.
Featuring state-of-the art projection and sound,
Milwaukee Film selections are sure to astound.

7

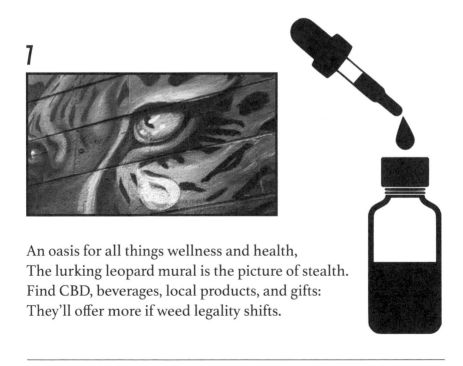

An oasis for all things wellness and health,
The lurking leopard mural is the picture of stealth.
Find CBD, beverages, local products, and gifts:
They'll offer more if weed legality shifts.

8

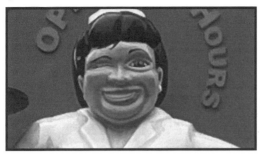 

A classic diner with a menu for days,
Rebuilt after the building was set ablaze.
Family-owned, they've redone the space,
Open 24/7, it's a favorite meeting place.

9

Once upon a time, just a dark and dirty alley,
Some spray paint plus talent, now an art gallery.
The frog above stands guard at the entrance;
Over 20 murals, it deserves more than a glance.

10

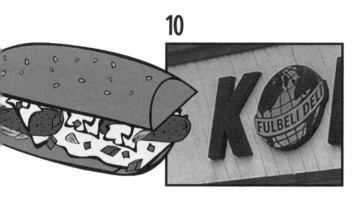

A deli with creative sandwich offerings,
With video game consoles, nostalgia's the thing.
Browse the fine beer and wine selection,
You're sure to find something for your collection.

11

Family-owned for five generations,
Their thin-crust pies are perfect creations
On a one-way street to pizza paradise.
Take my word: you don't have to think twice.

12

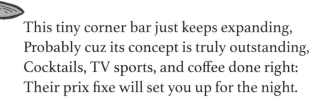

This tiny corner bar just keeps expanding,
Probably cuz its concept is truly outstanding,
Cocktails, TV sports, and coffee done right:
Their prix fixe will set you up for the night.

_____

_____

13

We've all had a night here we'd like to forget,
Cheap drinks, hopefully, haven't put us in debt.
The striped awning promises '80s music and decor,
Surprises can happen on that sticky dance floor.

_____

_____

14

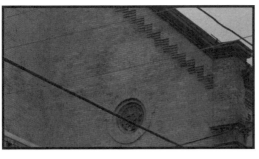

Milwaukee's celebrated priest presides over Mass
At this holy spot with impressive stained glass,
A Catholic parish that's one out of three,
Even non-Catholics, I'm sure would agree.

15

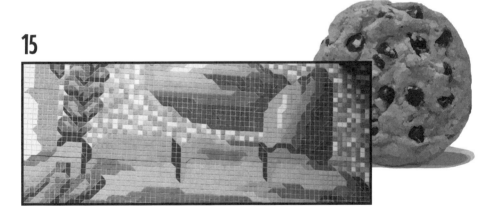

Their cookies or seeded rolls: which are more famous?
We love our carbs here. Really, can you blame us?
This bakery's been around since 1947;
Try the cannoli. Mmmm, I'm in heaven.

16

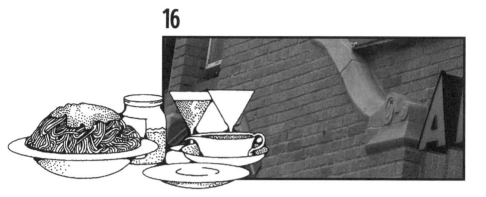

At the original site of a beloved Italian grocer
Is a new, popular concept to bring you closer
To mastering the cooking of true Sicilian dishes;
Feel like part of the fam: fulfill your wishes.

17

Climbing up a pipe, three creatures made of steel,
The sight might surprise you and make you squeal,
One of the many pieces of art in the neighborhood.
A (painted) rat, reindeer, and dragonfly look good.

18

Under the bridge, a unexpected spot for fun:
The clever use of this space is second to none.
Kids and adults can take a moment to swing
Before you hit up any of the neighboring things.

19

If you're seeking a dinner that's fit for a king
Or a spot to present someone special a ring,
The chef and cuisine here win much acclaim,
For 30-plus years they've been on top of their game.

20

A sumptuous feast from the Middle East
At a spot imposing, to say the least.
Lounge upstairs, there'll be room to spare;
Hookas and belly dancers, always there.

21

Marking this district, a steel tube on high;
The bright yellow diamond will catch your eye.
Apartments, riverwalk, and fresh market;
A place like home when you want to park it.

22

This hidden gem is the ultimate dive bar;
Their bumper stickers are on many a car.
Dimly lit with loud music and games to play;
Be like the locals: sit down and stay.

Lakefront

Milwaukee's Lakefront is the place where the city goes to play. Find beaches, bluffs, boats, and the iconic Milwaukee Art Museum, all at the shores of Lake Michigan. There are opportunities for recreation (and relaxation) all year long, but the Lakefront really comes alive in the summer with live music, festivals, boats, bikes, and more. This tour runs down Lincoln Memorial Drive.

1

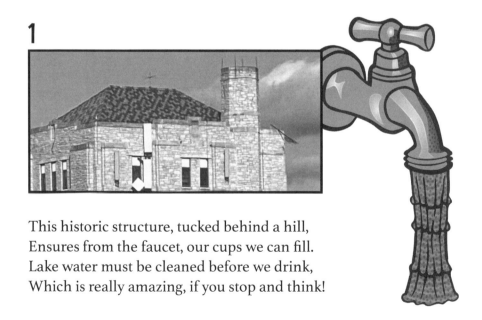

This historic structure, tucked behind a hill,
Ensures from the faucet, our cups we can fill.
Lake water must be cleaned before we drink,
Which is really amazing, if you stop and think!

2

This mansion's best-known for its immaculate garden,
Now it's a museum: trespass and ask for pardon.
Its Italian Renaissance style honors decorative arts,
The courtyard and the grounds are off the charts.

_____

_____

3

Are you seeking volleyball, swimming, and sand?
Or perhaps you just want to get your skin tanned.
There's a tiki hut if your throat gets dry:
Look up to see military planes fly by.

_____

_____

4

This famous stand serves both hot and cold treats,
Wisconsin's best indulgences, that can't be beat.
At the bottom of the hill and right next to the beach,
The name changed, but the menu, same for each.

_____

_____

5

Known for its coffee that's nice and strong,
This cafe's prized patio is open yearlong,
The Flushing Station once sat on this spot:
Look across the street and you'll see yachts.

_____

_____

6

At the bottom of the Brady Street Bridge stand three monoliths,
Red granite modeled after Chinese artifacts, or is it a myth?
At the top of the path, see another piece of this trio
And a beautiful spot to watch people come and go.

7

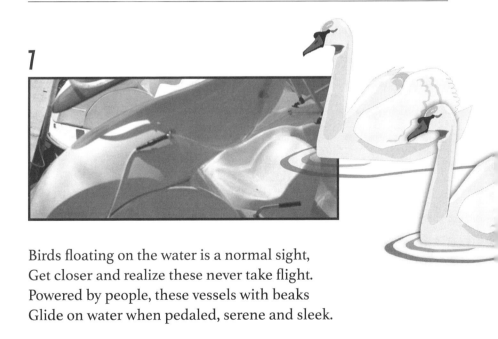

Birds floating on the water is a normal sight,
Get closer and realize these never take flight.
Powered by people, these vessels with beaks
Glide on water when pedaled, serene and sleek.

8

Learn how to navigate Lake Michigan by boat,
The kind powered by wind, if you'd like to gloat.
It takes skill and practice to master the sport
(Quick question: which is starboard and which is port?).

9

If you like to see objects take flight,
Look up, where the sun shines bright.
Known for their festivals and many fun things,
Grab a snack and select an object with wings.

10

Four letters spell a special word
That brings delight whenever it's heard.
This time, LOVE marks a special part
Of a building filled with beautiful art.

11

Like taking a vacation to Cape Cod,
Sit back and let yourself be awed
By the view of the lake and fresh seafood;
Happy hour here will improve your mood.

A work of public art covered in stainless steel disks
Creates colorful reflections when the wind whisks.
Look up to see seven big columns standing tall
As each and every onlooker, they enthrall.

13

Behind the museum's a round gathering place,
The perfect outdoor spot for a talent showcase.
Sometimes there's live music, or a tall ship on display,
Or just hang out and watch boats on the waterway.

14

The events held here are the absolute best:
These grounds have seen every type of fest.
Named after a mayor who served the longest,
The excitement for the music is the strongest.

15

On Lake Michigan, a park beyond compare;
Walk behind the festival grounds, if you dare.
Year round sec bikers, runners, fishermen;
Prairies and lake views will help you find zen.

East Town

The east end of downtown Milwaukee is the arts and culture hub of the city. Anchored by the iconic white "wings" of the Milwaukee Art Museum, this sector of the city is home to theaters, galleries, upscale eateries, and like most everywhere else in the city, great parks.

1

Irish hospitality is warm, not garish;
This charming inn and bar is a spot to cherish,
Offering authentic cuisine you'll want to savor:
Wash it down with a pint, do yourself a favor.

2

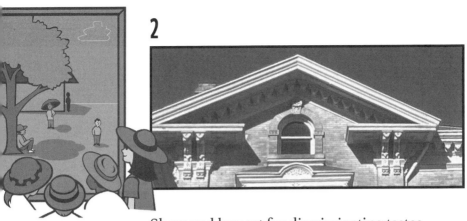

Show and buy art for discriminating tastes
From artists both local and internationally based
In this historic mansion, housed for over 50 years:
Their wide range of art is truly without peer.

3

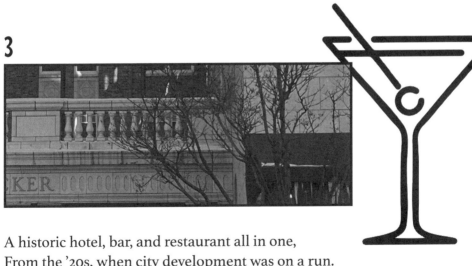

A historic hotel, bar, and restaurant all in one,
From the '20s, when city development was on a run.
The green awnings look casual, but the lobby is luxe;
Trust your gut and try it out, if your decision is in flux.

4

He stands in a park overlooking the lake,
He's cast in bronze, so he won't break,
A discoverer, son of Erik, and pride of Iceland,
This gesture to honor him is well-deserved and grand.

_____

_____

5

An homage to Milwaukee's first mayor, in this park
Also bears his name; it really hits the mark.
For his great contributions to establish the city,
To honor him, he was given a statue quite pretty.

_____

_____

6

This Art Deco hotel is a hidden treasure
Whose vintage cafe has flavors beyond measure,
The courtyard and counter, the best spots to sit.
(Keep coming back, and your pants might not fit!)

_____

_____

7

What happens when women come together to lead?
They help build community with their good deeds.
This club is a place to meet and to plan
Fundraisers and parties: together, yes, we can!

_____

_____

8

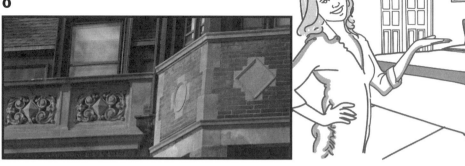

A double-sided mansion, turned boutique hotel
With a modern flair, and restorations done well,
Each room is unique, as are exterior details,
Proof, if you need it, that good craftsmanship prevails.

_____

_____

9

Looking for the best wings to share?
Look no further than Cathedral Square.
Swanky cocktails mixed with casual food
Are the ticket to get you in a good mood.

_____

_____

10

This is the oldest gay bar in the state,
At the top of everyone's list, it rates.
A bit hidden, search for the rainbow flag;
The bartender might be dressed in drag.

11

This family-owned restaurant serves great gourmet food
With culinary excellence, but no attitude.
The black-and-white striped awnings are so inviting,
And the staff, who will prepare items to your liking.

12

This is a place for all veterans to gather
And revive patriotism or, if you'd rather,
Remembering those who sacrificed
Fighting for freedom, not thinking twice.

13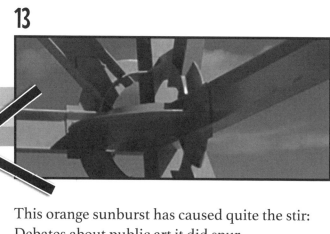

This orange sunburst has caused quite the stir:
Debates about public art it did spur,
Found in front of the famed museum "wings"
Made from I-beams, typically industrial things.

14

A place where kids let their imaginations soar,
With dozens of exhibits, they'll never be bored,
Interactive experiences with Milwaukee brands,
With all of this, your kids are in good hands.

15

This newest addition to Milwaukee's skyline
Is made mostly of glass, reflecting sunshine.
Equally attractive, a gathering place
A respite, allowing all a slow pace.

Downtown

Commerce and recreation meet downtown in Milwaukee. Historic buildings have stories to tell, so look closely: there are many magnificent details in the towering facades. Find the best of both casual and fine dining, museums, hotels, and even a rotating sculpture exhibit dressing up the streets of downtown.

1

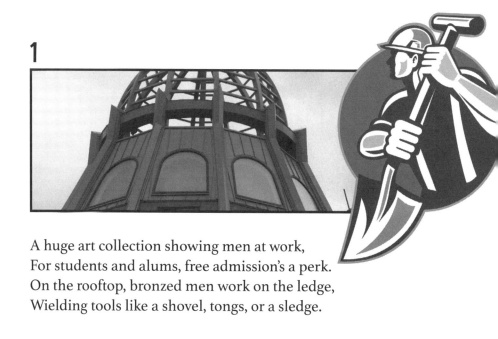

A huge art collection showing men at work,
For students and alums, free admission's a perk.
On the rooftop, bronzed men work on the ledge,
Wielding tools like a shovel, tongs, or a sledge.

2

Established by German immigrants in 1846,
See a gorgeous mosaic outside, done in bricks.
Three bells named Mary and the tower clock
Stand out when approaching the busy block.

3

A home for city government to plan and meet,
Hard to miss at the corner, it spans the whole street.
The massive copper bell tower is a sight to behold,
The building is gorgeous, if not covered in scaffold.

4

Meet up at this spot for a cup of joe
Or get some fresh air while awaiting a show,
Best-known in the winter for its slice of ice,
Skate rentals and cocoa on-site: twice as nice.

_____

_____

5

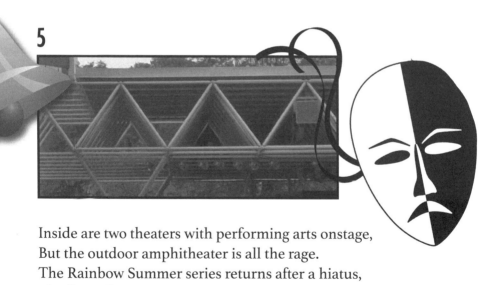

Inside are two theaters with performing arts onstage,
But the outdoor amphitheater is all the rage.
The Rainbow Summer series returns after a hiatus,
Thrilling all ages, in case you didn't know the latest.

_____

_____

6

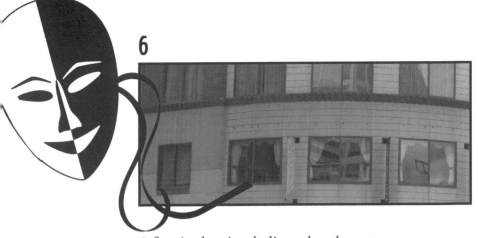

A first in the city, dedicated to the arts,
With lodging and dining, beauty in every part.
Stay to celebrate or just to be inspired,
Each room is comfy, especially if you're tired.

7

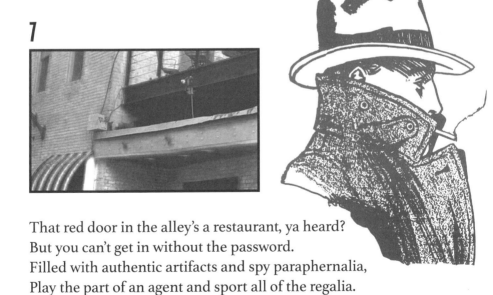

That red door in the alley's a restaurant, ya heard?
But you can't get in without the password.
Filled with authentic artifacts and spy paraphernalia,
Play the part of an agent and sport all of the regalia.

8

This large granite building on the main drag's hard to miss,
Not just a courthouse, but post office: did you know this?
Romanesque Revival style with arches on the facade,
Its tower stands tall, and many passersby it has awed.

9

"When the flame is red, warm is ahead," goes the rhyme,
Just like Milwaukee's weather, it's changing all the time.
A weather beacon atop this Art-Deco building is bold:
It warns, "When the flame is gold, watch out for cold."

10

The first men's social club this region had ever seen,
Because of its exclusivity, you may not have been,
Surely, you've noticed its handsome red exterior,
Its wrought iron-capped tower looks so superior.

11

Milwaukee's only four-star hotel that hosts celebrities,
Known for its great service and luxurious amenities,
A large collection of Victorian paintings, it boasts
(Though some swear its halls are haunted by ghosts).

12

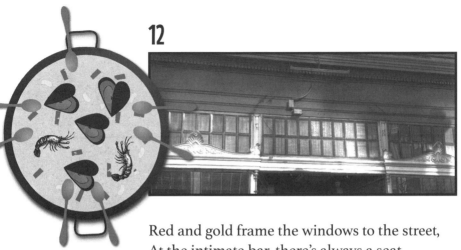

Red and gold frame the windows to the street,
At the intimate bar, there's always a seat.
Specializing in flavors from Portugal and Spain,
New menu each week, so go back again.

13

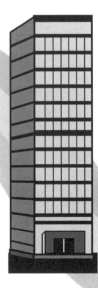

Three red, spotted bugs dot a stark facade,
Most people will agree, it looks rather odd.
It once housed a dance club named after them,
Mostly office space, but still considered a gem.

14

This historic building is home to a comprehensive gift shop,
Selling all the best Milwaukee products, so be sure to stop.
Once the Chamber of Commerce and Grain Exchange,
All gone, but the beauty of this impressive building remains.

_____

_____

15

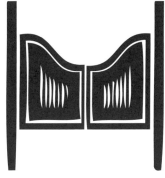

A saloon and eatery small, but big on charm,
Enjoy a drink, a friendly barkeep twists your arm.
Try their famous Friday fish fry of cod;
A menu so delicious, you'll applaud.

_____

_____

Westown

The west side of downtown has become the entertainment district, home to the new Fiserv Forum arena, the Miller High Life Theatre and the UW–Milwaukee Panther Arena. Just west of the Deer District, the historic Pabst Brewing complex has been redeveloped and honors our city's brewing roots by mixing old and new. Take a stroll on the Riverwalk to access breweries, boats, and even spot the infamous Bronze Fonz. Don't forget to take a selfie with him: it's a Milwaukee must. Start at the Wisconsin Avenue bridge and head west.

1

One of Milwaukee's most opulent places for a show,
All kinds of entertainment, crowds packing the cozy rows,
Named for its location right next to the Milwaukee River,
Forewarning: if you walk by at night, you'll catch a shiver.

_____

_____

2

Although many bronze sculptures dot the riverwalk,
There is only one that symbolizes hope in this flock,
Dating back to a sweet story from World War II
Of a mom and babies, now showing a patinaed hue.

n t p **3**

r s

i A writing machine invented right here?!
Find the marker near the District, Deer,
The first model, it wrote only in caps;
Its sound is familiar, a series of taps.

4

This Art Deco theater hosted Vaudeville acts
With great acoustics and opulence: those are the facts.
Vacant since the '90s, it's been left to crumble
'Til the MSO saved it; we are grateful and humbled.

_____

_____

5

Upscale food court, and bar and a place to play,
This spot features dining in a whole new way.
Once home to the city's grandest shopping mall,
This historic place hides many secrets in its walls.

_____

6

Yet another theater in this cool neighborhood,
It has the most seats and the acts are quite good,
There's something to see for every crowd,
Enjoy a High Life in your seat: make MKE proud!

7

Walk through this outdoor museum, of sorts,
Commemorating stars in Wisconsin sports
A row of bronze plaques with a famous face,
In WI, athletic prowess we embrace.

8

"Sound mind and sound body" is the slogan for this group,
In a historic building, they use the climbing wall to recoup.
The ballroom hosts concerts, weddings, and forums,
All are welcome to learn, and no need for a quorum.

_____

_____

9

A place to learn about Milwaukee's storied past,
So you can spout some local knowledge when asked.
The regal building sits at one end of the park,
When it comes to preservation, they hit the mark.

_____

_____

10

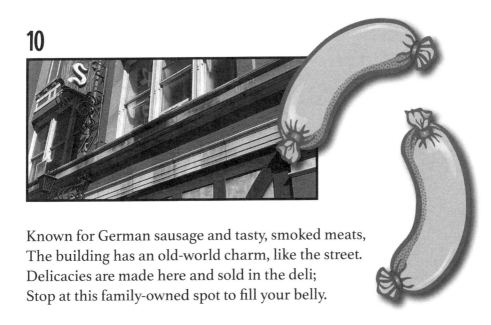

Known for German sausage and tasty, smoked meats,
The building has an old-world charm, like the street.
Delicacies are made here and sold in the deli;
Stop at this family-owned spot to fill your belly.

11

Among the oldest buildings on Third Street,
Now a saloon and eatery: stop in, take a seat.
The 72-foot bar is its claim to fame,
The perfect place to catch a game.

12

Right on the river, this green space has it all:
A rotunda, sculptures, and colored leaves, come fall,
Discovered and named for a French Jesuit missionary,
There's free concerts in the summer, when the nights are airy.

13

This arena is fit for NBA champs and stars,
Surrounded by a plaza and plenty of bars.
If you're not a fan of basketball, you should still go;
The music and shows are done by the pros.

14

For events where you need a ton of space,
Want to see it all? You'll have to pace.
A place for like-minded folks to convene,
Can't imagine how they manage to keep it clean!

15

Home to King Gambrinus, icon of beer,
You may have been to an event or tour here.
It's the former corporate office for Pabst Brewing
Restored to preserve its history, and worth viewing.

16

The new kid on the block, shiny and white,
A restaurant and more that fills up at night,
Using local ingredients to craft unique brews,
It's hard to decide which flavor to chose.

In a small urban park, neighborhood developers stand
Cast in bronze, they're immortalized hand-in-hand,
Granite rocks stacked high create a unique wall,
Relax and seek shade, once the trees grow tall.

18

When called for jury duty, you go here,
Part of the process, no need to fear.
The huge edifice, made from limestone,
Among architects, it's very well-known.

19

There are over 2.6 million items on display,
On a rainy day, let your kids loose to play.
Try the dome theater to feel totally immersed
Or the butterfly garden for a humid burst.

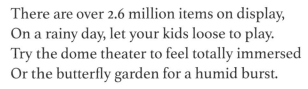

20

This spot had a rooftop restaurant that spun,
Many can recall it as an evening of fun.
At night it lights up, like a UFO in the sky,
It was recently renovated, so give it a try.

21

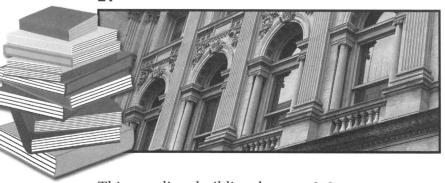

This grandiose building dates to 1898,
It's a landmark and resource for the entire state,
Filled with millions of books and interesting things,
Always free for county residents; a smile it brings.

22

It's called the big red church, they say,
Two towers, one in green and one in gray.
It's a place of worship, or you can see a show,
Comedy or drama, through the back you go.

23

This was the first public monument in the city
Depicting the first US president, looking so pretty.
It shares its name with the one at the National Mall,
Cast in bronze and lifelike (but not quite as tall).

Marquette/Avenues West

Further west of downtown is Marquette University's campus. It's a private, Jesuit school with a strong legacy of leadership and service. Beyond the university is a mixed bag of cultural and historic spaces that hearken back to a different era of our city. Don't miss these oft-forgotten stretches of Wisconsin and Michigan avenues, for there is much to discover! Start on Clybourn Street before crossing over to campus.

1

If classic, comfort food is what you seek,
This corner spot is open seven days a week,
Serving breakfast, lunch, dinner, and cocktails,
Due to its reputation, nostalgia prevails.

2

With a permanent collection and rotating exhibits
To inspire and teach creativity, and never inhibit,
Look for the blue diamond centered on the facade:
The styles on display are impressive and broad.

3

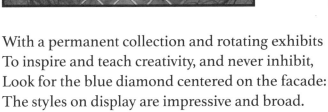

The spiritual center of the Marquette community
Hosts vigils and protests for equal opportunity.
First built over generations in a French village,
Moved to NY then MKE, amassing serious mileage.

4

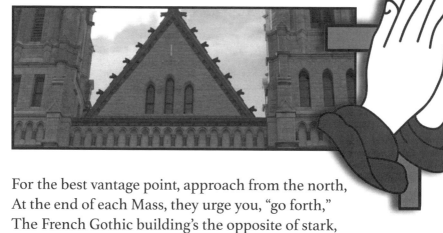

For the best vantage point, approach from the north,
At the end of each Mass, they urge you, "go forth,"
The French Gothic building's the opposite of stark,
So, in 1975, it was designated a landmark.

5

From the street it will catch your eye:
This vibrant artwork stretches high.
On the side of a building, four females,
Adorned with gorgeous and diverse details.

6

One of the first immigrant groups in the city
Has this place to gather and sing a ditty
Promoting all their culture, not just song,
So that their traditions continue strong.

7

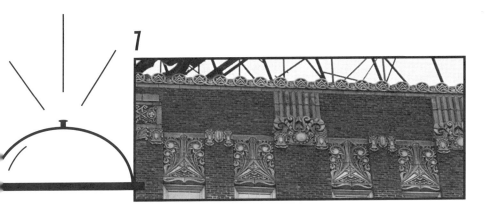

The yellow rooftop sign shines bright,
For locals and travelers, a welcome invite.
A fine example of Art Deco style,
This charming spot will make you smile.

8

This historic building has prominent window arches;
It's hosted everything from boxing matches to marches.
Now, it's mostly music, five venues total,
Bringing in all best bands, both national and local.

9

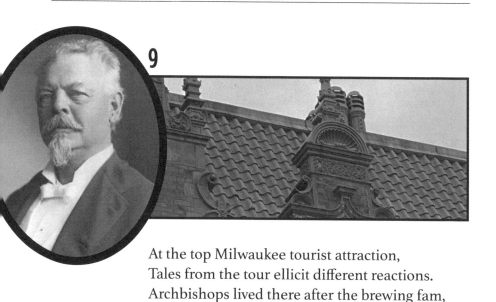

At the top Milwaukee tourist attraction,
Tales from the tour ellicit different reactions.
Archbishops lived there after the brewing fam,
The historic restoration is an ongoing program.

10

Wisconsin made famous the supper club;
This one is known for its succulent grub.
For a while there, it went by a different name,
But the top-notch service is still the same.

_____

_____

11

Dedicated and kind, this fraternal organization
Is housed in an ornate, outstanding creation.
A replica of one of the wonders of the world,
They also host a circus, see batons get twirled.

_____

_____

Historic Third Ward

If you're a tourist in Milwaukee, start your journey in the Third Ward. This historic warehouse district was once a hub for Italian groceries hawking fruits and veggies. Now, it's home to art galleries, boutiques, and the Milwaukee Public Market. The Hop streetcar takes visitors to and from the Ward, but once you're there, you'll find it's one of the most walkable areas in the city. Start on the east end of the Ward, near the festival grounds.

1

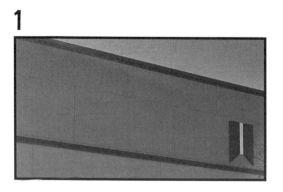

"Ciao bella!" You might hear some say,
Inside their courtyard, waste the day
Learning, eating, drinking, and playing,
This hangout's where you'll want to be staying.

2

A new tall building, black and sleek,
Inside those windows, take a peek,
Both a school and a performance space,
With people moving their bodies with grace.

_____

_____

3

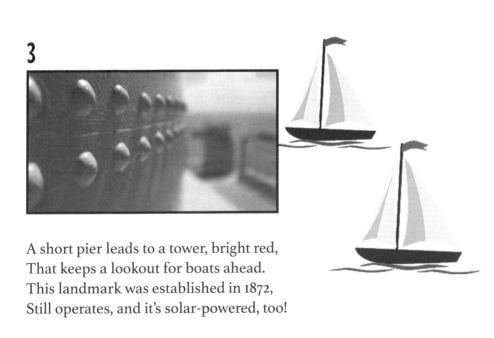

A short pier leads to a tower, bright red,
That keeps a lookout for boats ahead.
This landmark was established in 1872,
Still operates, and it's solar-powered, too!

_____

_____

4

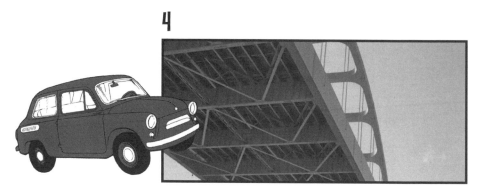

Golden arches, connecting two freeways,
It can even light up when a song plays.
Named after a mayor, it's a visible landmark:
You must see its illuminated colors in the dark.

5

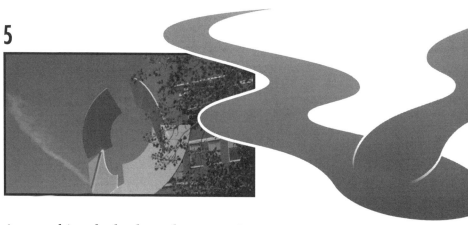

Approaching the harbor where two rivers meet
Is a bright public space, close to the street,
By a restaurant, bordered by Aspen trees,
Take a seat and enjoy the fresh lake breeze.

6

A rusty old structure out in the water
Looks like it could be home to a squatter.
It once was a useful part to the railway,
In front is a small park where you can play.

7

A school where creativity doesn't lack,
Bright colors are used, in front and out back,
Catch one of their shows for inspiration
To help with your own artistic creations.

8

In Catalano Square, a landmark that's round,
When it's running, there's a relaxing sound.
Whatever you do, don't take a drink;
Put your feet in the grass and let yourself sink.

_____

_____

9

With the look of an European opera house,
Powerful performances may cause you to rouse.
Don't be fooled, the big building looks a bit plain
Staging comedy and drama, but music's the main.

_____

10

A piece of public art showing appreciation
For all those who served at that station.
Look for the red brick and overhead door,
The sculpture remains where once was a store.

11

A place to rest your head after a journey
Or grab a bite if you're in town for a tourney,
The rooftop bar has the best views of the city:
The buildings and the lake look so pretty.

12

Best known for Bloody Marys and its brunch,
It's a great place to go for drinks that pack a punch,
People often overflow to the corner block:
If you get drunk, the passersby will gawk.

_____

_____

13

A new addition off one end of the market
Is a place to escape your woes and park it
With a tropical drink and oysters in-shell;
Pretty soon you'll be feeling swell.

_____

14

Want a career in the beauty industry?
Learn here how to appeal visually
Or get pampered at a discounted rate
With a head-to-toe makeover: don't hesitate!

15

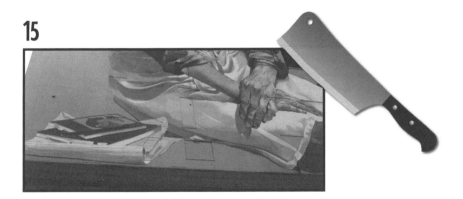

An anonymous person painted on the side
Of a historic building where fabrics were dyed,
This grand artwork depicts a female butcher.
Let's see more female leaders in our future!

16

A public space by the river for fun,
Try this paddle sport, no need to run.
This pair of hard courts under the highway
Is the place to release the stress of the day.

17

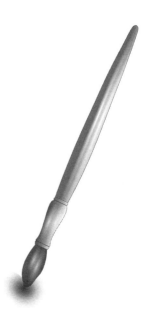

A great location to work, if an artist;
Sometimes collaboration's the smartest.
Stop and visit studios on Gallery Night
Leave with a snack: a late-night bite.

18

A historic brick building covered in greenery,
Like many bars, has familiar indoor scenery,
Dimly lit, comfy bar stools, and a spacious patio:
Grab a cocktail and tell the barkeep your woes.

19

tka, Illinois. Milwaukee's I
had chartered the grand
special Chicago benefit tri
to purchase new weapons.
or Alexander Randall, an o
ederal fugitive slave law,

Homage to a maritime disaster
From Chicago, a ship sank with its master.
Preserving history, are signs like these
Remind there's more to our state than just cheese.

On the Hop Streetcar

The Hop is Milwaukee's newest form of transportation. The sleek and modern streetcars operate on fixed tracks on the street. The 2.1 mile M-Line connects the Third Ward, downtown, and East Side neighborhoods. Best of all, it's free to ride, thanks to sponsor Potawatomi. New lines are in the works to connect even more of the city. Hop on the eastbound train at the Intermodal station to ride the 45-minute M-Line loop.

1

Not the only city's work by a man from Spain,
For his designs he's garnered worldwide fame.
This suspended structure goes to a new 'hood;
As a catalyst for redevelopment, it's quite good.

2

In an alley, a bright spot filled with folks,
You'll even find one guy who smokes,
But there's no smell, cause it's just paint;
From the others, you won't hear a complaint.

3

Look up to see a coveted view,
Dine and drink beer: from a boot, too!
Celebrate the cuisine of western Europe,
Enjoy beignets doused in chocolate syrup.

4

This shop is a standout on the block,
Its yellow storefront will make you stop.
Filled with large aisles that run deep,
Look closely, to see a lazy cat creep.

5

A charming, Art Deco spot to retire for bed
Or dine, if you're not ready to rest your head,
On a central, busy street with lots to do,
A rooftop patio offers a downtown view.

6

Hosting genres of music all across the board,
Its eclectic programming has won awards.
Under the red awning, the alternative frontier:
Did you know it was broadcast from here?

7

Intertwined bronze towers reach for the sky
In this famous spot that's caught your eye,
But do you know the real meaning or the name?
Circle it for new perspectives: the sculptor's aim.

8

A place to prepare for what lies ahead,
The cross on the building may have misled.
Kids study here and commit to attend college;
Good opportunities come with knowledge.

9

Celebrating the cuisine of this Asian nation,
Try the food and return without hesitation.
In a nondescript spot, set amongst housing,
It also hosts parties, with joyful carousing.

10

This historic spot, in Gothic Revival style
Has served the community for a very long while.
If you're curious and seek spiritual development,
This is the place for your days to be spent.

11

Empowering women to develop as a whole,
Getting into a good college is the main goal.
It's a place of faith, a cross on the facade;
The range of experiences offered is broad.

12

At the turning point of the route, a square
With a large piece of steel, darting into the air.
Finding this clue is the easy part,
But can you name this work of art?

13

Designed in an austere German style,
This landmark building's been here quite awhile.
Built with Cream City brick and a rounded steeple,
This parish offers programs and services for all people.

14

This message comes across loud and clear:
Turn around and look up, and it will appear.
The central image mimics a Civil Rights photo,
Using bold colors so the movement will grow.

15

Bringing new life to ugly concrete walls
On a square building with parking stalls
Are two bright and backlit automobiles:
This funky installation has major appeal.

16

This historic building was a communications hub;
Parallel towers still house part of the tech club.
With modern upgrades to its historic charm,
Secrets remain, but no need for alarm.

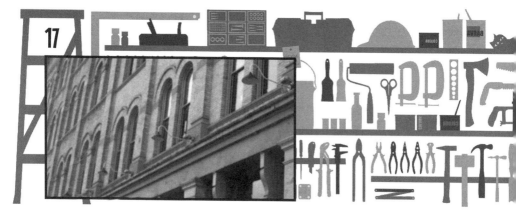

17

Rows of arched windows span its side,
It's six buildings in one, all big and wide.
Once a hardware store selling all types of goods,
Now it sits 'twixt two popular neighborhoods.

18

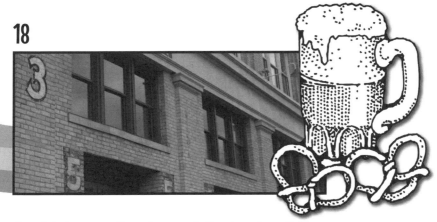

Combining two favorites: pub food and craft beer
And Cream City brick, all things we revere,
Look for the door between the numbers five,
Ride the Hop so you don't drink and drive.

19

A roaster instructs: slowly sip:
And soon you'll feel that caffeine zip.
Tour and learn more about the craft,
They even have cold drinks on draft.

Walker's Point

This industrial district is quickly becoming the city's new go-to spot for nightlife and dining, including the city's first food truck park. Walker's Point caters to everyone, especially members of the LGBTQ community and craft beer aficionados. While the district honors the neighborhood's Mexican roots, there is also a strong and growing Latinx presence. Start your journey on Water Street and head south.

1

It's a shrine for this specific type of doll,
You probably own one if you like baseball.
Want to know the history or how to get one?
Come to MKE for an afternoon of fun.

2

Using the airwaves to unite the community,
The studio space is appointed beautifully.
Stories and music are a catalyst to empower
Diverse people and groups, featured every hour.

3

Once the largest four-faced clock in the world,
The Saudis created one and its record was hurled.
This company created an automation boon:
History dubbed it the "Polish Moon."

4

A speakeasy, masquerading as a repair shop,
Order a milkshake, with whipped cream on top.
Or pick up supplies at the adjacent grocery,
With nostalgia, junk food, and liquor, mostly.

5

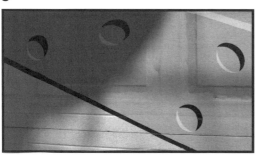

The Packers first created this fashion craze;
Watch it being made: you'll be amazed.
Who knew those squishy foam things were made here?
They make anything, even a coozie for your beer!

6

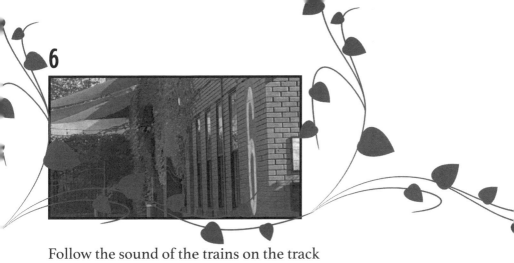

Follow the sound of the trains on the track
To the large patio and bar that's in back.
The brick is green, the garage door lets in light,
See the ballroom where couples dance all night.

7

One of the first to offer shared plates,
This style of dining is great for dates.
Their variety of gourmet, global cuisine,
Will transport you to places you've never been.

8

An unmarked brown door under the railway
Is where people gather to build and display.
It was first built to operate as a bridge station,
The longest-running club of its type in the nation.

_____

_____

9

Community gardens to enliven the block,
Marking the entrance is one giant rock.
It's a piece of art, but some may disagree;
This eco-arts learning center has lots to see.

_____

_____

10

In the dairy state, known for its rich custard,
This other milky treat has purists flustered.
It's yummy and smooth, in so many flavors,
Change your allegiance and throw in the waiver!

11

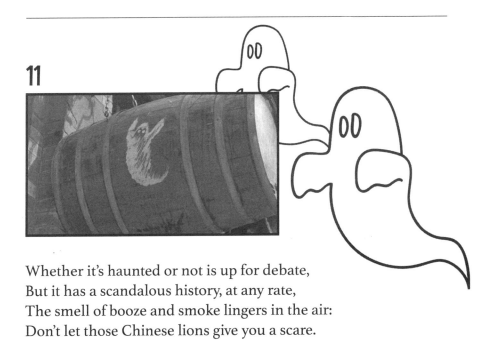

Whether it's haunted or not is up for debate,
But it has a scandalous history, at any rate,
The smell of booze and smoke lingers in the air:
Don't let those Chinese lions give you a scare.

12

Mmmm . . . can you smell those bitter beans roasting?
Marked with red, it's accustomed to hosting
Markets, weddings, and live music for all,
Bring your laptop, sit down, and work for the long haul.

13

On a busy commercial street is a center to learn
Design, technology, or a trade that'll help you earn.
The campus is huge and a Trojan, their mascot,
A gift from big donors, whose renovations it bought.

14

This Jesuit parish serves the Hispanic South Side,
Mass is in Spanish and Catholic rules abide,
The three arched doorways and dark gray brick.
With steeple features turquoise bands, quite thick.

15

Still a busy intersection, in an area once fraught,
A huge mural commemorates a protest in that spot.
On the corner, the gorgeous shop will catch your eye,
Once a pharmacy, now serving the tastiest pies.

16

Have a burger with a drag show on the side;
If you don't know how to act, let the host guide.
Weekly shows, bingo, and a rooftop patio,
Careful: the bartenders let neon liquor flow.

17

A bright work of art up high in the air,
When the sun is out, it creates an intense glare,
By night, the stained glass shines from the inside,
Panels create a mosaic, some skinny, some wide.

18

On one corner of the roundabout, it towers;
It's easy to relax on their patio for hours.
Tailored towards travelers on two wheels,
To anyone who loves hospitality, it appeals.

19

A comprehensive, sprawling tribute to this machine
And famous company, long a leader on the scene,
Find art, history, apparel, restaurants, and more,
So much to see and do; it will never be a bore.

20

This trailblazer was the first to distill spirits right here,
To their pledge to use local products, they adhere.
They make almost everything, except wine and ale:
Take the informational tour or just enjoy a cocktail.

21

Covered in bright murals, this brewery and taproom
Crowdsources recipes, some bad, you'd assume,
But they are all tasty, in their own unique way,
When the garage doors are open, it's time to play.

22

Like tacos served on a paper plate?
This no-frills spot is sure to satiate.
This little rabbit is a local mainstay,
The authentic mole will blow you away.

_____

_____

23

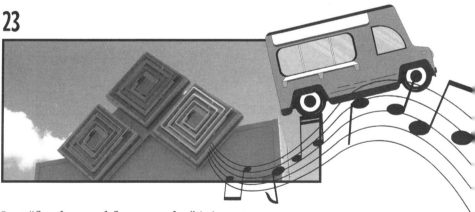

Just "food served from trucks," it is not
A mix of cuisines in a large gathering spot
And a place where everyone belongs,
Stop by for games, dances, and songs.

_____

_____

24

In this Square, a school, gallery, and more
For the community, this is the core
Not only for those born speaking Spanish
Support it or this resource will vanish!

_____

_____

25

A space for artists to learn and show work,
Pretty building with membership a perk.
Known for exhibit on Day of the Dead,
Art and creativity fill your head.

_____

_____

26

Different events in each of its spaces,
The very best from Spain it showcases.
Edifice not a hotel, per its name,
Warm and welcoming all the same.

_____

_____

Harbor District

Major developments are underway at Milwaukee's inner harbor, at the confluence of Milwaukee's three rivers (Milwaukee, Menomonee, and Kinnickinnic). This neighborhood is highlighting all that's great about Milwaukee's waterways. Recreation, research, and industry—it's all happening in the Harbor District. The best way to explore the harbor is by boat, but if you're on foot, start on South Water Street, just beyond the bridge.

1

If you have a boat, but not your own dock
To put it in the water here, people flock
Right where the river and the lake meet:
This public access, you just can't beat.

_____

_____

2

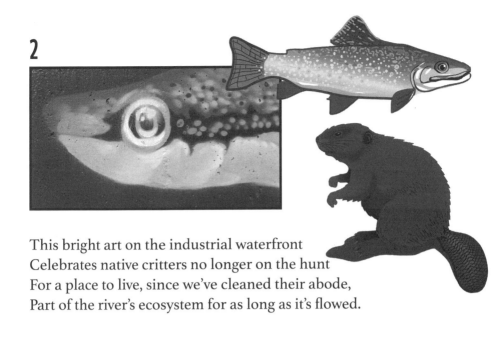

This bright art on the industrial waterfront
Celebrates native critters no longer on the hunt
For a place to live, since we've cleaned their abode,
Part of the river's ecosystem for as long as it's flowed.

3

Named for two great American pioneers,
This spot pours Old Fashioneds and also beers,
Sharing its lot with a taco truck and boats,
Learn how to maximize location, take notes.

4

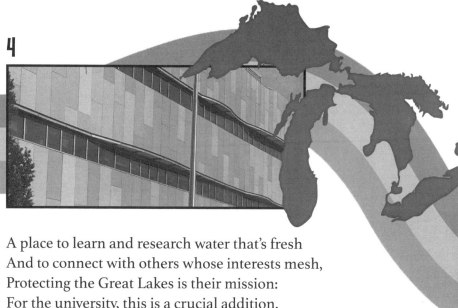

A place to learn and research water that's fresh
And to connect with others whose interests mesh,
Protecting the Great Lakes is their mission:
For the university, this is a crucial addition.

_____

_____

5

A place to jump, climb, slide, and play
At the end of street on a major waterway.
Miss it if you don't cross under the tracks;
New, it makes up for what the area lacks.

_____

_____

6

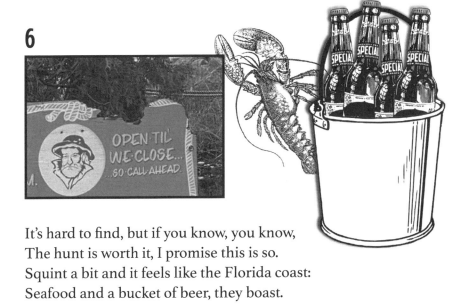

It's hard to find, but if you know, you know,
The hunt is worth it, I promise this is so.
Squint a bit and it feels like the Florida coast:
Seafood and a bucket of beer, they boast.

7

In a big red warehouse, find craft spirits,
Organic and small-batch are its merits.
Take a tour to learn about the long process
Or enjoy a cocktail like a vodka press.

Bay View

Equal parts trendy and old-school, Bay View has become one of the most desirable residential areas for young professionals and families because of its affordability, large green spaces, tight-knit community, and proximity to bars and restaurants. South Shore Park hosts one of the city's best farmers markets in the summer and fall. And the two-mile commercial corridor on Kinnickinnic (KK) Avenue appeals to collectors as well as those seeking locally made products. Take the iconic Hoan Bridge south and head as far east as you can go without falling in the lake.

1

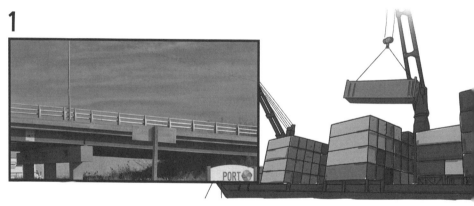

A less sexy part of the city, but essential,
As a global trade hub, its leadership's influential.
Hard to access by car, it's under the highway,
Messages of commercial impact it conveys.

2

This station close to the lake provides safety
And rescues boaters who've traveled too hasty
When cruisin' on the lake with your friends,
Or you'll pay the price to make amends.

3

Off the beaten path, Serbian food served proper
In a vintage building with a Schlitz globe topper,
Family-owned and operated for three generations,
Preserving the culture of their European nations.

4

This deli-grocery has been here since 1913;
These days, a market like this is rarely seen,
Boasting the best Italian imports of all kinds,
There's even a bar in the back to unwind.

5

Under the striped awnings, a lounge so chic
With dim lighting and vinyl booths that squeak,
The red glow makes everything look so fun,
Or is it the ice cream drinks and bowls of rum?

6

For over two decades, this club sans frills
Hosted tons of live acts, providing thrills.
See a band here first before they get big,
It's a national act's most intimate gig.

7

Want the best view of the skyline and lake?
With a cold local brew, a day it can make.
Grab a picnic table and a bite to eat;
Behind the pavilion is the place to meet.

8

This white house was a gathering place
For European immigrants seeking grace.
Big on charm, it remains a great resource
For history buffs, and a community force.

9

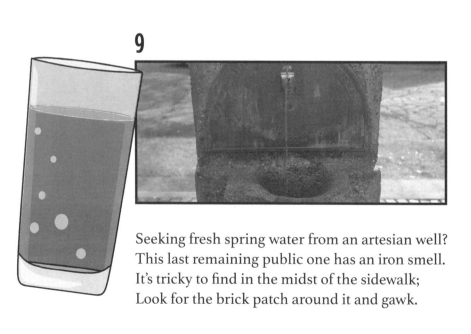

Seeking fresh spring water from an artesian well?
This last remaining public one has an iron smell.
It's tricky to find in the midst of the sidewalk;
Look for the brick patch around it and gawk.

10

This Catholic church is in the heart of Bay View,
If you need a reason to attend, here are a few:
Their work fostering community is meritorious,
The gold-domed steeple and cross are glorious.

11

Art and music intersect at this hip cafe,
The staff is so friendly, they'll make your day,
Their neon sign lights up the busy corner,
A haven for creatives, they host performers.

12

The gold lettering will draw you in,
But think before you ink your skin.
The artists here are truly talented
And, with tats, their bods are blanketed.

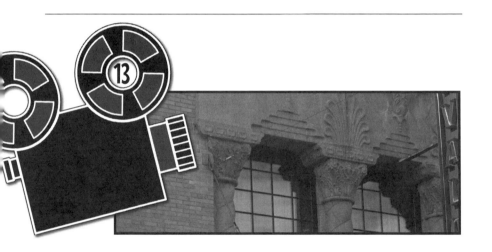

The building and sign are so opulent,
It's a unique experience, I'm confident.
Catch a fine flick, prop your feet, and rest,
Rumor has it their popcorn's the best.

14

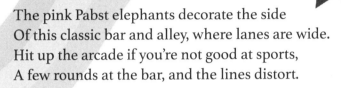

The pink Pabst elephants decorate the side
Of this classic bar and alley, where lanes are wide.
Hit up the arcade if you're not good at sports,
A few rounds at the bar, and the lines distort.

15

Seek out the glass window with the tiger,
It has quality home goods and decor.
From the outside you see the boho vibe,
It's a great place to find gifts for your tribe.

16

Not Clifford, but he is a dog, big and red,
He helps rescue those in situations of dread.
He stands watch next to the fire station,
To show appreciation, he was a donation.

17

Find the red awning with a mural above
If watching Euro soccer's what you love.
Grab a beer, relax, and get rowdy with friends,
At places like these, the fun never ends.

18

Whether a true connoisseur or just a beer snob,
The long line of taps will make your heart throb.
Right off the main drag, find the hot pink sign
Which shows a tree's fruit, not from a pine.

_____

_____

19

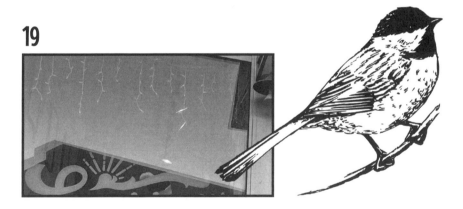

These two boutiques share the same name,
But if you didn't know, you're not to blame.
One has clothes and the other, local goods,
Named for an animal you'd find in the woods.

_____

_____

20

More public art on this big building off KK
With a wonderful message, if I may say,
Find everything needed to ride two wheels:
To most everyone, this lifetime sport appeals.

21

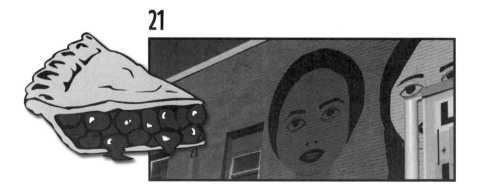

At the triangle intersection, the best spot for pie
And soups and sammies and drinks, oh, my!
A mural of diverse women look on from above,
For more the 20 years, a spot everyone loves.

22

Climb the colorful stairs to learn letterpress,
Try it with friends, you're sure to impress,
They create posters, invites, and cards
So that you can send your best regards.

23

When summer comes, want to chill on a hill?
A spot with music that wishes you will.
With a pond, playground, and beer garden too,
This place is best enjoyed when skies are blue.

Historic Mitchell Street

Once the city's shopping district, Mitchell Street is now a mix of historic architecture, cultures, and community services. Soak in all the bright colors from new murals exemplifying diversity and traditions. Historic Mitchell Street is truly a main vein on the city's South Side. Start on Lapham Street and head south.

1

A swanky little lounge, Milwaukee's oldest,
No drink menu? The bar staff is the boldest.
On a residential block, it could be a house,
It's a great spot to rekindle with your spouse.

2

From the highway, see these two towers,
They're capped in gold, and show the hour.
The first urban, Polish parish in the US,
This one is so big, it's easy to guess.

_____

_____

3

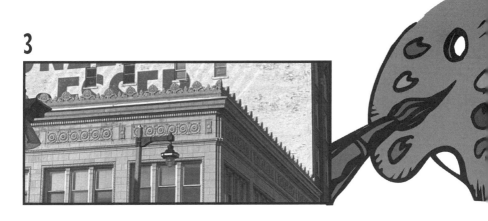

If you want a unique place to call home
In a huge historic building, where you can roam,
The big, open spaces draw artists of all kinds
To a community of people with like minds.

_____

_____

4

Visit the Middle East without leaving your seat,
Their flavors are authentic, they can't be beat,
The storefront is unassuming, but just trust me,
The family-owned spot helps Syrian refugees.

5

Named for a Polish actress, the marquee remains
Closed, but historic relics it still contains.
Film legends and musicians graced the stage,
A new owner it needs so it can reengage.

6

The largest in MKE, be sure to stop by,
Newly remodeled, with windows reaching high,
Once a place to shop, now get books for free,
If you walk by, people hard at work you'll see.

7

This health center serves a population in need
Of care in line with their own traditions, indeed,
With two-toned wood on top of concrete,
It occupies the entire corner of the street.

Lincoln Village

Another South Side neighborhood with plenty of history is Lincoln Village. Nostalgic spots and monuments pay homage to the neighborhood's first Polish settlers. Now primarily a Hispanic neighborhood, the mix of cultures is interesting and fun. Start at Beecher Street and veer east as you search for historic spots.

1

Everything's cuter when it's small:
In this case, we're running with the ball.
This corner tap has a secret in back,
Four lanes, not for driving, and a rack.

2

A replica of blessed St. Peter's in Rome,
Known for its large and impressive steel dome,
A place for holy sacraments and Mass,
Built strong by the Poles, so it'll last.

3

In the middle of the park, a tribute to him,
He was a war hero with vigor and vim,
Cast in bronze, dressed in uniform and all,
He was never one to back down from a brawl.

4

Expect to find things like meat and canned food,
But the selection of vodka is also quite good,
Importing only the favorite European stuff,
These comforts from home make life less tough.

5

Creative Mexican dishes from scratch,
Focusing on seafood and the daily catch,
The fresh, handmade tortillas are a draw,
Next to a market, try the ceviche, raw.

6

This shop builds steel frames
That bear Milwaukee's name,
Since 1928, family-owned and run,
Buy or rent one for a day of fun.

7

Many influential people rest here,
Including the barons that sold beer.
Over 200 acres, up the street,
So peaceful, stone sculptures replete.

Clarke Square

This active and vibrant community was once home to a large population of the Hmong, an indigenous people from southern China. Now the heart of Milwaukee's Hispanic community, Clarke Square is covered in bright murals celebrating heroes and peacemakers. The supermarket El Rey anchors the business district on Cesar Chavez Drive while Mitchell Park boasts flora and fauna from all over the world (inside those curious-looking glass domes). Start at 23rd and Mineral streets and then head east.

1

This spacious park is actually quite plain;
A playground, trail, and building remain.
It's a great spot for the community to unite,
Take your kids for a picnic and fly a kite.

2

A red brick building with a bright steeple
Is a place to worship with other people.
Primarily, they speak Spanish here
And most parishioners live quite near.

3

Five bright diamonds, surrounded by flowers,
On the side of a building, don't look for hours,
It's right on the main drag, a mural so bright,
You can probably see when you drive by at night.

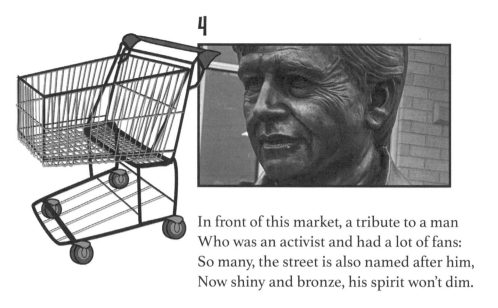

4

In front of this market, a tribute to a man
Who was an activist and had a lot of fans:
So many, the street is also named after him,
Now shiny and bronze, his spirit won't dim.

5

The phrase, "Si se puede!" or "Yes you can,"
Coined by this woman, when in a real jam,
Finally, a mural to honor her impact
On farm workers, when basic fairness lacked.

6

The Cream City brick home named for the man
Who made those same bricks, a trend he began,
Now an office for the neighborhood's leaders,
Creating change (not the kind in parking meters).

7

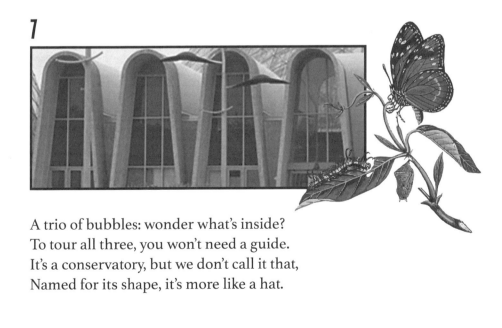

A trio of bubbles: wonder what's inside?
To tour all three, you won't need a guide.
It's a conservatory, but we don't call it that,
Named for its shape, it's more like a hat.

8

Bright paintings of people really stand out
On a historic building for a company with clout,
Now a place to serve those in need of healing,
Not just the body, but to sort out your feelings.

9

Against royal blue walls, its name in silver letters,
A place where kids go to ensure their future is better
With a work-study program and prep for higher ed,
Developing spiritually, while filling their heads.

10

Hands-down the best burger on this side of town,
In a quaint pub, I promise, it won't let you down,
Look for the white building with the neon sign,
Take out or have a beer and stay to dine.

_____

_____

11

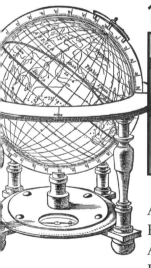

A place to search for relics from the past;
Find quality items all built to last.
A tall, red brick building has three floors
Filled with rare items, unlike other stores.

_____

_____

Menomonee River Valley

Sometimes just called "The Valley," this area on the bed of the Menomonee River is home to some of the city's largest attractions. Aside from baseball, bingo, and bikes, the Hank Aaron State Trail is one of the city's largest intra-urban trail systems. Focused on both economic and environmental sustainability, the redevelopment of this neighborhood continues with craft breweries and a design corridor. Start on Emmber Lane, just north of the Menomonee River.

1

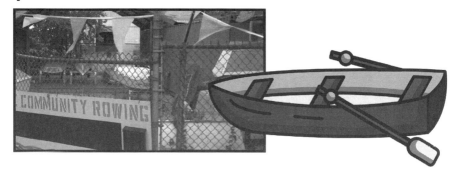

Want a great spot to get your feet wet?
Get a boat in the water: they help, don't fret,
It's a great way to see a calm MKE waterway,
But only use boats without motors, okay?

2

Follow the bright green arrow to a big, open lot,
Walk further to find the gold nectar—jackpot!
The huge production and tasting room
Opened during the height of the boom.

3

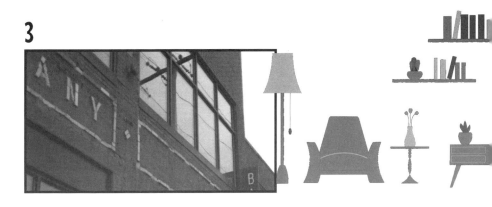

A third-generation, family-owned biz,
Tons of comfy places to sit, there is.
Peer inside through glass garage doors,
Let them decorate, if you find it a chore.

4

One of the original Schlitz taverns, now a pub
And a grill serving burgers and other grub,
Famous for their huge, crazy Bloody Mary,
So loaded with fixins, it's hard to carry.

5

It looks like just a warehouse, but inside, a surprise:
A showroom with thousands of lights, prep your eyes,
Find quirky or elegant fixtures for all styles,
Rows and rows of hanging bulbs go on for miles.

6

Working steel tanks on display behind the bar,
Right on the river; from the city, it's not far,
In a historic building that used to make lights,
To sample a few, try one of the beer flights.

7

Whether you prefer two wheels or four,
Here's a place where you can shred and score
Advice from pros, or just go to observe,
These sports sure do take a lot of nerve.

8

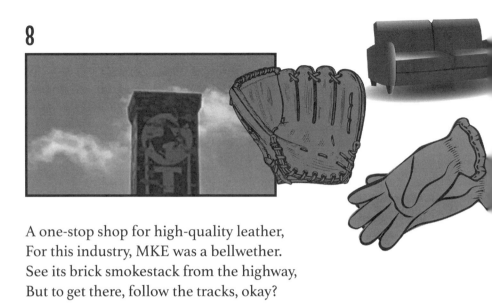

A one-stop shop for high-quality leather,
For this industry, MKE was a bellwether.
See its brick smokestack from the highway,
But to get there, follow the tracks, okay?

9

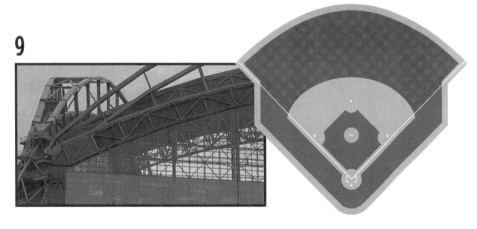

Recently renamed, home to the same team,
The guys on the field are living their dream.
The retractable roof is a main draw,
It takes the winter forever to thaw.

10

A replica Italian village at the roundabout,
Creating foods so good, you'll want to shout,
Using family recipes, available in the freezer,
Their crispy pies will turn you into a believer.

_____

_____

11

A 14-mile path connecting east to west,
The views of the city are simply the best,
Named after a famous baseball player
And record breaker who ignored the naysayers.

_____

_____

12

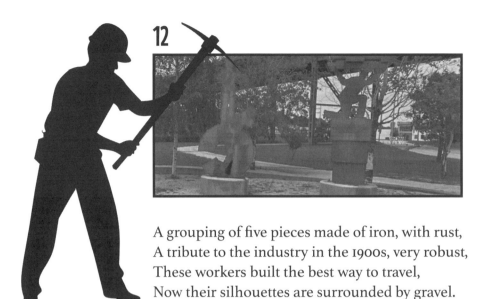

A grouping of five pieces made of iron, with rust,
A tribute to the industry in the 1900s, very robust,
These workers built the best way to travel,
Now their silhouettes are surrounded by gravel.

_____

_____

13

This cross-legged man with a perfect patina
Sits in front of something, as big as an arena,
But this building has much more colorful flair;
The clue is the name of the guy with long hair.

_____

_____

14

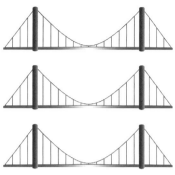

A very literal name for a recreational spot,
Native plants and flowers cover this plot,
Paved trails perfect for jogging and biking,
The city views from high points are striking.

15

Depicting the diversity and history
Of this area, study the artwork to see.
Then pass through the tunnel and up
To a nature center then fill your cup.

Washington Heights

If you want a combo of city and suburbs, Washington Heights is the place to be. This cozy community just west of the city has a sprawling Olmsted-designed park (of New York City's Central Park fame), corner bars, and coffee shops. Most of the action is on Vliet Street—approach it from Washington Boulevard, so you don't miss the first spot.

1

A statue of this founding father is at one end
Of this huge spot: over 100 acres it extended
Best-known for the bandshell and summer concerts,
A lagoon and nature center, too, on the outskirts.

_____

_____

2

For over 50 years, they know how to fill
Bellies with a decadent meal off the grill.
Don't forget to end the meal with custard,
And to your custom burger, add mustard.

3

A wide-open space to play different sports,
You'll even find people learning on the courts.
With a huge playground, it's a great spot for kids,
Come summer, its everyone's favorite digs.

4

Pop in to this shop for something living,
Or find a perfect gift for the giving,
Get delicate blooms for a special event,
Or greenery, if you don't like the scents.

5

We all know the secret to great 'za is the crust,
And gourmet, high-quality toppings are a must,
It's all about their fermented, hand-stretched dough
And the extremely hot oven, creating a char below.

6

Get a fresh, roasted cup of joe
And grab a pound or two to go,
It's a crucial part of the a.m. routine,
Their giant logo ensures they're seen.

7

Part of a trio of historic cinema gems,
You have to visit each one of them.
This one has an Art Deco feel,
Screening only classic reels.

8

Famous characters decorate the entrance,
Of the interior, a mural creates a semblance.
The only remaining shop like this for kiddos,
Experts at mixing illustrations with prose.

9

Aim for a spare, strike, or even a turkey,
Enjoy, even if you think, "This isn't for me."
This sport caters to families looking for fun,
Remember to trade shoes in when you're done.

10

This urban oasis is the spot for a hike,
A place to appreciate nature, if you'd like,
It teaches students about the outdoors
And it also fosters a love to explore.

11

It feeds the neighborhood fish during lent,
And requests all sinners pray and repent.
Admire all details on the ornate facade,
In Latin, the cornerstone pays tribute to God.

Wauwatosa

Commonly called 'Tosa by the locals, this neighborhood has the best of all worlds—plenty of residential, commercial, and green space. Located immediately west of downtown, there are several different districts to explore, and a bustling farmers market in the village center in the summer and fall. Start on State Street for some classic Milwaukee history, just before you enter Wauwatosa.

1

On the famous brewing company's grounds,
Find a mysterious area that's not always found,
Follow the signs next to Miller Inn and descend
To the historic storage spot, if a tour you'd attend.

2

Approaching 'Tosa proper, find the very best meat,
Grass-fed and pasture-raised, quality can't be beat,
Look for the giant mural of the cow's parts
That reminds good butchering is truly an art.

3

Their mozzarella sticks are their claim to fame,
But anything deep-fried in Wisco gets acclaim,
This favorite sports bar also serves BBQ,
It gets packed with fans of the Brew Crew.

4

Itching to get crafty but need an assist?
Stop here with friends, they'll give you the gist,
Have a drink at the bar and let creativity flow,
Take home something that you're proud to show.

_____

_____

5

A popular hangout with killer wings,
They also serve a burger fit for kings,
Look for the pergola and for the green sign,
Join their rec sports teams for a good time.

_____

6

Across the train tracks, a place to play,
Skate, hit, jump, or watch the clouds all day.
Music and events when the weather warms,
And that little splash pad, where the kids swarm.

7

Not many stores left anymore
With customer service at their core,
Connect with other literary lovers,
And never judge a book by its cover!

8

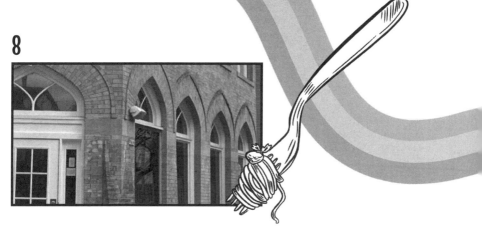

The original spot for a restaurant group in town,
Right on the corner before you head down,
With authentic Italian fare and a charming patio,
A great place to celebrate and let the wine flow.

9

Vive La France, especially its cuisine,
You have to visit, if you've never been,
The vibe here practically whisks you away,
The menu's filled with all the mainstays.

10

Listen up, Four-Eyes! If you want to look hip,
Stop here in the Village on a busy strip
For a wide selection of modern frames
And a staff that backs up all their claims.

11

A cute spot to unwind and imbibe,
There's monthly clubs to subscribe,
Pour your own glass from a machine,
Red or white, you can taste anything.

12

It's just like the Wisconsin Dells, only smaller;
To keep your kids close, you'll have to holler.
With a playground and popsicles right on-site
It's a perfect summer day, stretching into the night.

13

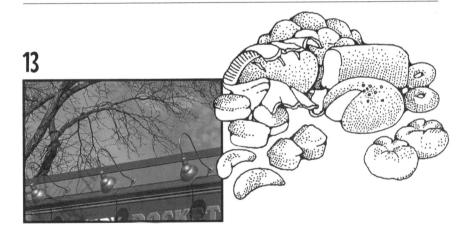

Carbs, crafted with painstaking detail,
Kneading and loads of butter it entails,
Artisanal methods create the great taste,
You'll love every bite: not a crumb you'll waste.

14

It's always abuzz on Saturday morning,
See the line outside as it starts forming,
Everyone wants the best cruller in town,
None of the confections will let you down.

15

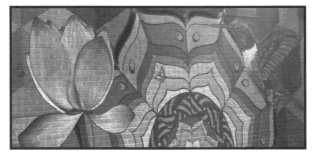

Look for the bright mural or spinning pole,
Preserving a classic tradition is the goal,
It's a place to freshen up, relax, and feel good,
Look super-sharp and discuss manhood.

16

Their big screen, couches, and beer can transfix,
Showing the best cult classics and also new flicks,
The dark, painted brick sticks out on the street
And the neon sign and marquee just can't be beat.

_____

_____

17

Look for the green sign and the red bag,
They have 13 stores, but they won't brag.
Find a deli and gourmet groceries aplenty,
When you leave, your cart will be far from empty.

_____

_____

18

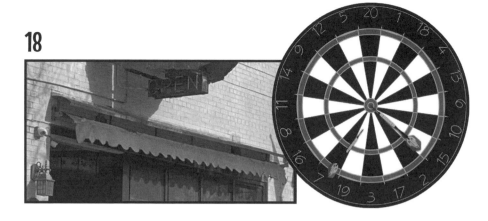

This quintessential dive bar is old and small:
Down a cold one or throw darts at the wall.
The charm remains and there's stories to be told,
Grab a pizza next door and let the night unfold.

19

Boasting a comprehensive selection,
Imbibe, no matter your predilection.
The upstairs growler gallery is lesser known;
Due to rare finds, its popularity has grown.